MW00901913

Authentic Communication

20 CONCRETE PRACTICES TO ENHANCE YOUR COMMUNICATION & JOY

Your Communication Workbook

WORK
WISDOM

KEDREN CROSBY, MPS

SARAH COLANTONIO, MS

© 2018 Kedren Crosby and Sarah Colantonio

All rights reserved.

Illustrations by Sarah Colantonio

Design by Modern Art: www.itsmodernart.com

ISBN 978-1-387-52372-6

Dedication

To all of our bosses (authentic and inauthentic).
Thank you for teaching us what matters most.

Table of contents

ACTIVITY!

Color the picture to the right of the United States Postal Service worker and the hip Googlers below.

The reason we have them here together is they both have come to learn the immense value of **Authentic Communication** in the workplace, and they learned it in vastly different ways.

Introduction

THE POSTAL SERVICE had to learn about Authentic Communication the hard way. You might be old enough to remember the origins of the phrase "going postal." The story is that in the mid-1990s there was so much frustration within the ranks of the United States Postal Service that it would cause some employees to resort to violence. Repeated episodes of alarming assaults by postal workers occured. The frustration had a lot to do with the ways that communication happened within that culture. The culture was built on the style of the military and so the communication patterns were often barking orders or even using intimidation techniques in order to convey the urgency of a task. There was little effort to save face or even build rapport within interpersonal relationships. While those techniques work for communicating in the military, they didn't work so well since the Postal Service is populated by civilians. It got so bad that Congress intervened and talked to the Postmaster General and essentially said, "You must come up with some way to fix the communication patterns so that people stop hurting each other."

"Project Redress" was piloted in the post offices in Florida. They worked to create communication patterns and practices that would help management and employees seek to understand each other's ultimate interests, collaborate, and become less autocratic. It was so successful that it was replicated throughout the country and it was quickly found to save money and lots of organizational pain and suffering. The well-being of the employees improved along with retention. The Postal Service learned about Authentic Communication but they learned about it the hard way.

Google wanted to find out why some of their teams were so high performing and others were merely "meh." If you want to know more about this, google the article on Google in the New York Times called "The Quest for the Perfect Team." At first, when they sliced and diced the data, they couldn't find what the secret sauce was. They

Welcome to Your Communication Workbook.

Here at Work Wisdom we are honored to bring these 20 communication practices to transform your workplace. Timing is everything. This workbook is designed to be absorbed at a rate of one section per week so as to give enough attention and space to each practice. We want you to try on the practices fully before you move on to the next practice. As you work through each section, you will be able to reflect on the lessons to determine what will work best for you and the people in your organization. We want you to be deliberate as you go through the chapters. The material we are sharing here will be transformative if put into action. As you progress through the workbook, keep in mind any questions or issues that might come up. Utilize our discussion board or our email addresses which are available on the Work Wisdom website (www.workwisdomllc.com) and we will be happy to answer any questions.

looked at age, sex, education and struggled to see what the connection could be. They would have given up but the CEO was adamant. Yale researchers came along to help Google do some more digging. They found that by creating teams where there is the ability to feel safe, they had better outcomes. They had more creative ideas. They had better rates of execution and they actually enjoyed working with each other.

Too often employees experience a lack of collaboration and overall poor communication in the workplace. The cost is not hard to calculate. Not only does it feel bad, it hurts our companies and organizations financially.

The Four Dimensions of Authentic Communication

Communication is the most essential skill we can wield as human beings. But we often take it for granted. Leaders spend 85% of their time communicating but only absorb about 25% of what they hear. The result? Organizational pain. When relationships lack authenticity, clarity, psychological safety and meaningful engagement, work is a nightmare. Relationships fall apart, projects fail, people get run down and unhappy.

For example, in the very masculine world of oil rigs, one of the problems was in that dangerous environment, an uncommon number of injuries or deaths were occurring. It took a third party to come in, assess the damage and realize that the culture of the oil rig was toughness above all else. If you didn't know how to do something, you didn't ask. Or if your buddy was killed in an accident, you soldiered on and went right back to work. When workers were given the opportunity to explore their feelings and become more vulnerable, to talk about what they were going through, the rate of accidents and deaths dropped dramatically. Emotion was finally acceptable (to hear more about this story, listen to *The New Normal* episode of the podcast, *Invisibilia*).

Similarly, individuals and teams uncover their original resourcefulness and creativity when communication is congruent, empathetic, conversational and self-regulated.

DEFINITION:

Authentic Communication is the artful practice of building productive, trustworthy and helpful exchanges. The Authentic Communication practices were culled from family therapy, Appreciative Inquiry, psychology and communication research. **Mindful communication, emotionally intelligent communication, psychologically safe communication** and **collaborative communication** are the four dimensions of Authentic Communication.

First, **MINDFUL COMMUNICATION** is reliant on deep awareness. It improves our focus and clarity in our work. There has been a lot of research published regarding mindfulness in the workplace. Work can be a source of strain and stress. But in David Gelles's book, *Mindful Work*, he notes the outcome of one corporate executive's experience with mindfulness training. "Employees felt more comfortable with themselves at work, more likely to pay full attention, prioritize tasks, get rid of unproductive activities, more focused overall, and self-aware. They reported dramatic spikes in their ability to focus on a project from beginning to end, be fully attentive in meetings, conference calls, and presentations and to notice when their attention has been pulled away and redirect it to the present." In our distracting world, learning how to pay attention is vital.

In the mindful communication section, you will investigate five concrete practices that help foster mindful communication in your workplace.

Secondly, **EMOTIONALLY INTELLIGENT COMMUNICATION** is communication which leverages the usage of emotional and social skills to enrich the outcome of the exchange with others. Emotional intelligence (EI) is how we perceive and express ourselves, how we build and maintain interpersonal relationships, how we cope with stress and use emotional data to solve problems and make decisions. Some research says that only about 6% of our professional success is attributable to IQ but 60-85% is directly linked to EQ. EQ is something you can tangibly increase. One very concrete way to invest in 'psychological capital' in our organizations (with up to 200% ROI according to Dr. Fred Luthans, father of Positive Organizational Behavior) is by enhancing emotional intelligence in the workplace.

Increasingly, EI is being used to improve and increase performance and outcomes for many industries. EQs are measurements of EI and can assess individuals or teams and recommend means of improving the performance of the individual, the team, the organization and the patient. EI is also used as a method for identifying leadership potential among team members and is increasingly used in hiring decisions.

You will explore five practices that help your communication become more emotionally intelligent in this section.

Thirdly, **PSYCHOLOGICALLY SAFE COMMUNICATION** is communication that builds safety for interpersonal risk-taking. In psychologically safe teams, members feel accepted and respected.

In Google's research on effective teams, psychological safety was the differentiator in terms of defining what made a team most effective in problem solving and innovation. It makes sense. If you feel accepted among your team members, you can risk suggesting a weird idea knowing you won't get shot down. Making a mistake doesn't result in punishment. Questioning authority is possible. In this section, you will learn practices to enhance psychological safety for yourself and your coworkers.

Lastly, the **COLLABORATIVE COMMUNICATION** practices are designed to harness the collective brilliance of a group or system. Chief among these tools is finding out how you manage conflict. If you discover that you typically hold out for what you want or conversely always let the other person "win" the argument, you might want to learn how to collaborate so that your interests AND the interests of the other are fulfilled. This is the sweet spot where conflict can spur innovative thinking and cement connection between the people on teams. Simply put, when you and your colleague have gone through the mud together, you come out much stronger.

ACTIVITY!
AUTHENTIC COMMUNICATION ASSESSMENT

Let's be honest with ourselves.

We want you to take a few minutes to consider how you communicate at work. Don't overthink your answers. This is not a scientific tool, but it gives you a baseline to help you reflect on your current usage of Authentic Communication.

Authentic Communication Assessment

Scale 1-5   1: Never   5: Always

___ 1. In meetings, I stay on topic no matter what.

___ 2. I refrain from crafting my response while the other person is speaking.

___ 3. I have gotten feedback from coworkers that I am a good listener.

___ 4. I learn from and about others by hearing what they have to say.

___ 5. When dealing with someone who is inauthentic, I speak less and listen more.

___ 6. I align my actions with my words.

___ 7. I back up what I say with evidence.

___ 8. I rarely if ever interrupt others during meetings.

___9. I wait until the information is clear before I make a decision.

___10. I believe that "cooler heads prevail."

___11. I check with my (partner/friends/co-workers) as a sounding board for reality checks on how things are going.

___12. I make a point of taking the psychological temperature of the room before and after meetings.

___13. I do unto others as they would have done unto them.

___14. I prefer to speak face-to-face when it comes to difficult conversations.

___15. I'm mindful of how much and what I contribute in a conversation.

___16. I adjust my behavior based on how the other person is feeling.

___17. I find it helpful to put myself in the shoes of my friends and my frenemies.

___18. When I run a meeting, I work with the participants to create norms for conduct and process.

___ 19. I adhere to established norms of behavior when it comes to meetings and overall communication.

___ 20. I assert myself when I disagree with a policy (instead of bottling it).

___ 21. I am able to freely brainstorm ideas.

___ 22. I rarely if ever talk about people behind their back in a destructive way.

___ 23. I say positive things about people in my organization behind their backs.

___ 24. I find out about and share the stories of times when my team did great work.

___ 25. I can hold others accountable without seeming judgmental.

___ 26. When I lead a meeting, I work to ensure that all participants have equal air time.

___ 27. I work to create bi-directional conversations with people at all levels in my organization.

Almost there!

Keep going, you're doing great

___ 28. I influence others by tailoring my argument in the terms and values that resonant with that particular friend or foe.

___ 29. I'm aware of my predisposition to managing differences (avoid, accommodate, compete, compromise or collaborate).

___ 30. I'm agile in adopting the conflict style which will optimally enhance my outcome.

My total score

120-150: My authentic communication is through the roof !

90-119 : My authentic communication needs some attention.

30-89 : My authentic communication needs to go to the emergency room.

ACTIVITY!

Where is your attention? Think about where and when you are paying attention while you fill out these questions.

I am most present when I:

I am least present when I:

I've noticed when I do this I am able to pay more attention:

THE FIRST DIMENSION

Mindful Communication

MAYBE MINDFULNESS HAS BECOME A BUZZ WORD because so many of us are in desperate need of it. We are moving at such a fast pace, it can feel overwhelming but also make the idea of slowing down and paying more attention seem ridiculous. What we do know is when we are fully engaged in our work or a relationship or whatever it is, we feel good. We feel centered. We aren't stressed or worried about time or what other people think. It's freedom. Being mindful isn't just doing yoga or meditating on a hill at sunrise, although that can be very nice. Being mindful can happen in our offices, in our kitchens, in our cars, in our everyday. Where is your attention? Think about where and when you are paying attention while you complete the activity to the left.

WEEK 1: THE PARKING LOT

WEEK 2: CONGRUENCE

WEEK 3: THE PAUSE PRACTICE

WEEK 4: MINDFUL LISTENING

WEEK 5: AUTHENTIC SELF-COMMUNICATION

Color the picture below of the
workers using the Parking Lot.

WEEK 1. THE PARKING LOT

"...I must stay on track to keep my purpose."
-ALICE WALKER

Have you ever been to a meeting that went long because you and the other members got sidetracked by topics NOT on the agenda? If there is a degree of psychological safety in your group, you are likely to be a victim of this since members feel comfortable sharing ideas and giving insight. That in itself is a wonderful thing and a key ingredient to high performing teams. However, constantly going off topic and going over time can be frustrating.

Sharing ideas and insights can be great, but constantly going off topic and going over time can be frustrating.

So how can we maintain psychological safety and innovative thinking without going off track? By using a simple mindful practice called **The Parking Lot.**

Label a whiteboard, flipchart and designate a parking lot "attendant". Any topic or issue not on the agenda can go on The Parking Lot to be discussed later. This way, the ideas can flow but time and schedules are respected and the meeting stays focused.

Remember, The Parking Lot is not a garbage can. Be sure to get the items in the Parking Lot delegated to the appropriate staff for execution. Some items in the Parking Lot may be useful items in the agenda for future meetings.

WORKSHOP THE PARKING LOT:

How will The Parking Lot enhance the focus and results of my team?

Here's a list of three meetings I lead or participate in that would benefit from The Parking Lot.

1.

2.

3.

How will I introduce and sustain this practice within these sessions?

What obstacles do I foresee in managing The Parking Lot?

Who might be an effective Parking Lot attendant during a meeting
(not the person facilitating the meeting)?

WEEK 2. CONGRUENCE

"I have long since come to believe that people never mean half of what they say, and that it is best to disregard their talk and judge only their actions."

–DOROTHY DAY

Every day, often several times a day, I watch the anguished face of someone as they tell me that they once truly believed in their leader/teammate. They share that ONCE, they would have scaled mountains for them. But that was all before their workplace-heart was broken by the insidious destroyer of teams and dreams: **incongruence.**

Congruence is the act of being aligned, inside and out. Your values are reflected in your words. Your words are reflected in your behaviors. You feel what you say, you say what you feel. You say what you do, you do what you say. You live your values consistently and authentically. We trust people who are congruent because they do what they say

> **DEFINITION:**
> **Congruence** is the act of being aligned, inside and out.

they are going to do. They follow through which makes us feel that they have integrity. We want to work for congruent leaders. We want to help congruent teammates and flourish on congruent teams. We want to marry congruent partners. We'd like to vote for congruent politicians, too.

Consider how your workplace would be different if everyone adopted the practice of congruence. Congruence is one of many Authentic Communication practices which builds a culture of psychological safety, innovation and high per-

formance. In an optimally congruent workplace, promises are fulfilled (without threats, cajoling or guilt!), employee engagement is healthy, communication is trusted and expectations are clear. This all leaves more time, money and political capital to expend on other interesting and even profitable activities.

How Can I Become Congruent?
How Can My Team Embrace Congruence?

❶ Being congruent requires **self-awareness** to understand your values, interests, principles, goals and yes, even feelings. Journaling, mindfulness, emotional intelligence development, the VIA, (Values In Action: www.viame.org) and creating your own personal core values are good places to start. Congruent people are keenly aware of their purpose. Become curious about yourself and take note of what you learn.

❷ Congruence requires healthy levels of **assertiveness and emotional expression** in order to convey interests in a constructive manner. Learn your own preferred style of managing conflict (which you will take in week 20 to glean your own style).

❸ Congruence requires **self-discipline**, too, as we must resist the urge to play fast and loose with the truth. Congruence also requires you to stay true to your word and follow through on promises. When you encounter that high school frenemy at the grocery store, tap the brakes before you blurt out, *"Yes, it's so great seeing you! Let's get lunch!"* The power of the Positive No can help you find the right words.

WEEK 2 ACTIVITY!

Color the picture below illustrating the concept of **Congruence.**

❹ Ask for kind-hearted accountability partners. When you fall out of alignment, you will get the much-needed tap on the shoulder or elbow in the ribs to let you know that you are human. Then, sincerely *feel* sorry, authentically say that you are sorry and intentionally change your *behavior* accordingly (which is all, congruent! Congratulations!).

WORKSHOP CONGRUENCE:

What beliefs are most important to me?

Dorothy Day said she stopped believing what people said and instead looked at what they did to know what they really believed. What actions align with what I believe?

What actions might misalign with what I believe?

What steps can I take to be more congruent?

What beliefs are most important to my team?

How do our words and actions align with our beliefs?

How can my team collectively take steps to be more aligned with what we believe?

THE PAUSE PRACTICE

WEEK 3. THE PAUSE PRACTICE

"The two most powerful warriors are patience and time."
-LEO TOLSTOY

"Adopt the pace of nature: her secret is patience."
-RALPH WALDO EMERSON

For those of us who are interrupters, before the speaker stops speaking, we're already formulating our response. When we don't listen fully to the entire thought of the person with whom we're communicating, we're losing about half of the information, the substance as well as the emotional (relational) content of the message. In this concrete, verbal way, we encourage you to pause before you formulate your response.

This may feel a little awkward at first because of the delay between when the speaker finishes and when your response starts. Others on your team will appreciate the fact that you listen the entire way through the conversation.

DEFINITION
"relational context of a message"
it's the underlying meaning of a message, the connotation. For example, you might ask your friend how she's doing and she puts on a smile and says tightly, "Oh, I'm great." You recognize that the relational meaning of "I'm great" is actually, "I'm terrible."

There is a second way we talk about The Pause Practice. Imagine getting an email and there might be some content that feels inflammatory, hostile or maybe even overly excited. You might want to freak out. Instead, take more time to reflect on it so you can create a better response. You know what those emails are. Remember, you can use your impulse control and delay your reaction to when you have more clarity before responding.

In this second way in which we use The Pause Practice, we're encouraging you to pause, use impulse control when communication has some negative energy behind it and needs to be managed in a mature fashion. We encourage you to spend time being reflective, seeking to understand before pulling the trigger and firing back a response that you might later regret. The Pause Practice is almost always highly effective in de-escalating hostile situations.

WORKSHOP THE PAUSE PRACTICE:

I recall a time when I did not pause and regretted my response. It was:

I recall a time when it was beneficial for me to pause before jumping to a conclusion or decision. It was:

What would have been the cost if I hadn't paused?

I am sometimes impulsive in the following situations:

WEEK 4. MINDFUL LISTENING

"If there is any hope for us, it lies in... reclaiming ourselves as a listening species."

-MARIA POPOVA (CREATOR OF BRAIN PICKINGS)

Brandon was working in finance in Chicago when he started taking pictures of strangers on the street. When he got laid off from his job, he moved to New York City. He continued to take pictures of people on the street but more regularly, as if it was his full-time job. Not only did he ask the people he encountered on the sidewalks if he could take their photo, but more importantly, he asked them questions about their lives. He chronicled what he saw and heard. The creator of *Humans of New York* gained millions of followers on Facebook and a book on the *New York Times* bestseller list. *"When I was younger, I thought listening was just about learning the contents of someone's mind. I'd always try to finish their thoughts just to show them that I knew what they were thinking. As I got older, I learned to listen better. I realized that by trying to anticipate their mind, I was ignoring their heart."*

Listening takes up a huge chunk of our communication. It's a vital and often untapped skill. In spite of the fact that listening to our partners, our children, our coworkers, and our friends would enhance our lives exponentially, we often ignore those around us. Valerie Martin, in the article, "Listening Is a Verb" said, "It would be astonishing to discover how many problems might be solved if only more of us would seriously and actively listen to those who are trying to communicate to us." Kevin Sharer, a biotech CEO shared how he started his career in his 30s as an arrogant and horrible listener focused on "intellectual winning" instead of comprehension. Sharer said that before his epiphany, his communication was about 90% telling and 10% listening. He realized that not only did it need to be closer to 50-50, he also needed a certain amount of humility to listen mindfully. Sharer acknowledged that most of us know that it's important to listen and that it's valuable but that it is often "more lip service than conviction. Listening can be learned but to change your behavior on any important dimension, you've got to have deep self-awareness. You have to change and you have to want to change." Like any practice, meditation, running, yoga, healthy eating, it takes discipline and motivation to become a better listener.

The significant benefits of listening might be some motivation to you.

❶ **You are more likable and trustworthy.** In one study of taped conversations, the individuals who spoke less were considered more likable. Not surprisingly, studies also show a positive relationship between listening skills and other social, cognitive and communicative abilities.

> **Like any practice, meditation, running, yoga, healthy eating, it takes discipline and motivation to become a better listener.**

MINDFUL LISTENING

❷ When you listen, you teach the other person to listen as well. This might take time, but the impact is inevitable.

❸ You seem smarter. You will actually be smarter because you'll know more. Studies also show better listeners tend to make more money and have higher positions in organizations.

❹ You will make fewer mistakes.

❺ You will be less stressed and that will make the people around you less stressed.

THE LISTENING CHALLENGES

To build our listening skills, yes, make eye contact, yes, have an open posture, yes, nod, yes, ask clarifying questions. But on a broader scale remember these points. Listening takes work! It is in no way passive. So number one, prepare yourself to listen. Eat breakfast, get a good night's sleep. Mentally and physically, prepare. Secondly, don't just listen for content. People lie. Or they say things they don't mean or they verbally agree when they don't really agree. So, listen for ultimate interests, motivations, emotion---go deep. Look for patterns. We repeat ourselves enough, don't we? Look for that. Lastly, exercise appreciative listening. Look and listen for ways to appreciate the way your team members speak, think. Are they good story tellers? Are they passionate? Persuasive? Funny? Eloquent? Listen for that and enjoy it.

Listening takes practice. The following listening challenges are designed to help concretely hone the ability to absorb, focus, and strengthen listening skills. When practiced, be aware they will definitely impact your relationships in remarkable ways. You will become a magnet.

Consider adopting one challenge per month or having a friend or partner who will take the challenge on as well.

1. The Lean-in-literally Challenge
Show physical interest and attention to the speaker using eye contact and overall receptive body language.

▶ Consider this survey taken with New York City hospital patients regarding 2-minute visits by doctors. All of the visits were two minutes long, but the doctors who stood to talk to the patients were perceived as spending far less time and not really listening. The doctors who pulled up a chair and sat next to the bed, looking into the patient's eyes, were thought to be truly interested in the patient and spending more time on the visit.

▶ Julia Wood's book *Communication Mosaics* retells the experiment where researchers taught a group of psychology students responsive listening techniques (eye contact, nodding, open posture, smiling) and had them try these techniques on a boring history professor who was infamous for reading his lecture notes in a monotone voice. After a few minutes of class, the students all kicked into high gear with their responsive listening techniques. It was as if this professor became an entirely new man. He blossomed. He got animated. He started to interact with them. But here's the kicker, after a certain point there was a preplanned signal and the psychology students stopped responsive listening and suddenly returned to slouching and passively taking notes. The poor professor tried to get them back for a few minutes but when they didn't respond, he went back to his monotone note-reading.

2. The iPhone Challenge

Put it away (physically and emotionally) when you are trying to connect with a "real-time" human.

▶ One of the greatest gifts you can give another person is your full attention. When a communication class was asked how they felt when they were really listened to, one student said, "I'm surprised." We are so distracted by our dinging notifications. How essential is that new email in our inbox or that someone commented on our Facebook post, or the number of likes on our Instagram or Twitter feed? It can wait. NPR sponsored their own related challenge: "The Bored and Brilliant Challenge" encouraged participants to keep phones in their bags or pockets while traveling. Look up, see the world around you. Truly listen to and look at the people around you.

3. The Pause Practice. Sound familiar? It is.

Don't interrupt. Let the silence work for you.

▶ In another study with doctors and patients, doctors interrupted patients less than 30 seconds into their description of their problem. If a doctor is meant to diagnose, how is 30 seconds or less going to give them the whole picture? It's not. The study had another iteration where doctors waited and let the patient's finish talking. The surprising finding was that on average, patients spoke for only about 90 seconds before stopping but it gave the doctors a far clearer picture of the cause of their patient's illness. On top of that, the doctors who allowed their patients to speak for 90 seconds were perceived to be more likeable and competent just by listening. Often our instinct is to jump in with our brilliance and not let other people finish their thought, but we miss out on their core interests and backstory if we finish for them.

4. Grow a Third Ear

Listen to hear the other's motivations, anxieties and underlying interests.

▶ This challenge requires the listener to tap into intuition, focus and attention. Theodor Reik, a Freud-trained psychoanalyst, wrote a book in 1948 which described how to understand and relate to others. By using observation and analysis that requires self-awareness and a deepened awareness of the speaker's interests and motivations, real connection can be achieved. Begin by listening to yourself and then branch out to others. Read between your own lines. Listen for themes. Hear the strength and emphasis of certain words and note sequencing and cadence. You will be surprised at what you learn.

Integrating the practice of listening into your everyday life can transform your relationship with yourself and others. It can lead to greater success in your work and home life. Give it a try. It takes 40 days to start a habit. Why not adopt the practice of mindful listening?

WORKSHOP MINDFUL LISTENING:

I am an exceptional listener when:

There is someone who I have trouble listening mindfully to. One thing that is interesting about this person is:

Three actions I will take to listen to this person more mindfully are:

1.

2.

3.

The best listener I know is:

My favorite person to listen to is:

They're my favorite person to listen to because:

WEEK 5. AUTHENTIC SELF-COMMUNICATION

"I think self-awareness is probably the most important thing towards being a champion."

-BILLIE JEAN KING

In order to reap the benefits of Authentic Communication in our workplaces, we need everyone to be authentic. Honest. Have high reality testing. Well, the question is, *"Do we tell ourselves the truth?"* You've probably heard about cognitive dissonance. This is the discomfort from holding two or more contradictory beliefs at the same time. Sometimes we're confronted with information that conflicts with our existing beliefs. We become what's called psychologically uncomfortable and we're motivated to try to reduce this dissonance and actively avoid situations and information which increase it. We want to see consistency between our expectations and reality. When we don't have the consistency, we actively work to reduce the dissonance by ignoring or denying information that conflicts with our beliefs. For example, I believe that I am a funny person. I like to believe that. It's a core belief of mine. Occasionally, data will come about that reflects that maybe I'm not as funny as I think I am. I will actively work to reduce the dissonance by ignoring that data or ignoring the person who is presenting that data, because I'm uncomfortable

psychologically with information that disproves my perception of my own identity. And probably you might be too. In order to get to real maturity and understand the complexities of other humans including ourselves, we have to become more comfortable with the dissonance, with the paradoxes, with the contradictory data.

Brené Brown, in her book *Rising Strong*, explains how arguments go with her husband when he's presenting data that is dissonant with her perceived version of herself. She has this very handy phrase that we encourage you to use, too. It helps to separate her perception of reality from real reality so that she's able to counteract the urge to reduce that dissonance. She begins her response to her husband by saying, "The story I'm starting to tell myself is that..." It depends on the argument and what data he's presenting to her of course, but maybe she'd say, "The story I'm starting to tell myself is that you don't respect me" or "the story I'm starting to tell myself is that you think I'm irresponsible." In my case, where I am looking at data that is contradictory to my own identity, I should probably use the phrase, "The story I'm starting to tell myself is that you think I'm not funny."

Byron Katie explains brilliantly in her book, *Loving What Is* how to ask a series of four questions to open your mind to authentic understanding. Authentic understanding is essential for communication.

DEFINITION

Cognitive dissonance:

The discomfort from holding two or more contradictory beliefs at the same time.

Here are Byron Katie's four questions:

1 Is it true?

2 Am I absolutely sure it's true?

3 How do I react, what happens when I believe that thought?

4 Who would I be without that thought?

These techniques help us consider our story from a different perspective, and shake loose from unhelpful beliefs or assumptions.

Another Byron Katie technique is called THE TURNAROUND

Our example is:
My co-worker doesn't respect me.

1 Turn around to the self: *I don't respect me.*

2 Turn around to the other: *I don't respect my co-worker.*

3 Turn around to the opposite:
My co-worker DOES respect me.

Then come up with 3 examples of each statement that confirm it as true.

WORKSHOP AUTHENTIC SELF-COMMUNICATION:

Three core identity traits I believe about myself are:

1.

2.

3

Sometimes I do things that are misaligned with the identity I have constructed of myself. An example:

The following is a disempowering story I tell myself:

Is it true?

Am I absolutely sure it is true?

What happens when I have this belief?

Emotionally Intelligent Communication

A GREAT MANY BOOKS AND ARTICLES have been written about emotional intelligence. Emotional Intelligence consists of the following four elements; **how we perceive and express ourselves, how we build and maintain interpersonal relationships, how we cope with stress,** and **how we weave emotional data into how we solve a problem or make a decision.** Emotionally Intelligent Communication uses these features to enrich the outcome of our exchanges. Emotionally Intelligent Communication requires self-awareness, self-regulation and the ability to recalibrate how we communicate feelings.

WEEK 6: CHECK-INS, CHECK-OUTS

WEEK 7: THE PLATINUM RULE

WEEK 8: SELF-REGULATION

WEEK 9: RICHNESS OF MEDIUMS

WEEK 10: EMPATHY AND DEEP PERSPECTIVE-TAKING

Color the picture below of the team members using the one-word Check-ins and Check-outs.

WEEK 6. CHECK-INS AND CHECK-OUTS

"Who questions much,
shall learn much,
and retain much."

— FRANCIS BACON

The One-word-check-in and One-word-check-out is an emotionally intelligent question that allows us to take the temperature of the team before or after a meeting. If the Check-in question is framed well, you can discern the energy levels and optimism at the meeting. The meeting facilitator begins by asking the participants to share one word (hyphens are used liberally here!) that is a truthful answer to the question framed by the facilitator. Often, questions are along the lines of, *"Describe how you're feeling about the strategy we're discussing today"* or *"Share one word that describes what strength you plan to bring to this effort today."* The greatest aspect of the One-word-check-in is that it breaks the psychological ice. When everyone on the team has already spoken in a meeting, it is much easier to speak up a second time once you're into the middle of the agenda.

Similarly you can take the pulse at the conclusion of the meeting with a One-word-check-out. Thoughtful framing of the question extracts the collective sense of the meeting. An example of a One-word-check-out question might be, *"Share one word that describes your most important take away from this meeting"* or *"What is one word that describes the most critical next step?"* Check-ins and Check-outs are conducted as a round robin (going around the circle) so that every member of the team has a chance to participate. By creating a team norm of Check-in or Check-outs, people come to expect and optimally use this tool for the energy of the group and the benefit of the team.

DEFINITION
One-word-check-in and
One-word-check-out:
An emotionally intelligent question that allows us to take the temperature of the team before or after a meeting.

WORKSHOP CHECK-INS AND CHECK-OUTS:

Here are three ways I can "take the temperature" of the people in a meeting before I dive into the content.

1.

2.

3.

I can use this information to enhance the outcome of the meeting in this way:

I can use this information to enhance the cohesion of my team in this way:

A helpful "check-in" question to ask at the next meeting I am leading:

A helpful "check-out" question to ask at the next meeting I will be leading:

WEEK 7 ACTIVITY!

Color the picture below illustrating a violation of the Platinum Rule.

WEEK 7. THE PLATINUM RULE

"Do not do unto others as you would that they should do unto you.
Their tastes may be different."

— GEORGE BERNARD SHAW

In a giant hotel conference room with over 200 people gathered to hear a popular mindfulness guru speak, I nervously listened to the instructions for an exercise. *"Find someone you don't know, stand face to face and ask them, what do you want? Continue to ask them until we let you know when it is time to switch. Go."*

I didn't know one person at the conference so I didn't think it would be difficult to find a stranger, but alas, everyone around me was pairing up so quickly, I was without a partner. Finally, a late comer dashed in and was paired up with me. I was relieved. She looked kind.

WEEK 7 ACTIVITY

Ask your colleague or your partner if they have a few minutes to conduct the following exercise:

Face each other.

Look at each other.

Person A asks Person B, **"What do you want?"**

Person B answers whatever comes to their mind.

Person A repeats the question.

Do this 5 times.

Then reverse roles. Have Person B ask Person A, **"What do you want?"**

As we started the exercise, I was amazed by how quickly we connected. *"What is it that you want?"* The repetition in questioning helped us go beyond surface answers. It gave us permission to explore within ourselves, *"What do I really want?"*

We know the Golden Rule and it is helpful. But imagine this: Do you drink coffee? If you do, do you have a particular way you like it? I do. I like a good bit of vanilla almond milk creamer in my coffee. Maybe you prefer iced coffee or you like it black, or just with sugar. Let's imagine that every day I come into work and bring you a coffee the way I take it. How long until you say, *"Sarah, please stop. The way you drink coffee is disgusting!"* Sure, I thought I was being nice, but I was applying my coffee preferences onto you.

The Platinum Rule posits that you do to others as they would want done to them. If I had used the Platinum Rule, I would have said, *"Hey, I want to bring you coffee tomorrow. How do you like it?"* and that would have made us both happy.

In order to collaborate or create mutually satisfying solutions to problems, you must become adept at the practice of asking, *"What do you want?"* and also, *"Why?"*

The What-Do-You-Want Exercise

Instructions: Ask your colleague or partner if they have a few minutes to conduct the following exercise

1. Face each other.
2. Look at each other.
3. Person A asks Person B, "What do you want?"
4. Person B answers — whatever comes to mind.
5. Person A asks again, "What do you want?"
6. After asking & answering 5 times, switch roles.

WORKSHOP THE PLATINUM RULE:

CIRCLE ONE: When I completed the "What do you want" activity, I knew what I wanted.

TRUE   FALSE

I said I wanted:

1.

2.

3.

4.

5.

CIRCLE ONE: It was   **EASY   HARD   GOT EASIER**   to say what I wanted.

CIRCLE ONE: It was   **EASY   HARD   GOT EASIER**   to listen to what the other person wanted.

They said they wanted:

1.

2.

3.

4.

5.

Self-regulation

vaguely hostile email

WEEK 8. SELF-REGULATION

"Elegance is refusal."

— COCO CHANEL

"Breviloquence: (noun); Speaking briefly and concisely

— WORDSMITH.ORG

If you really want to demonstrate respect for your co-workers, self-regulate. We all know people who don't have a filter. Self-regulation is the ability to monitor and control our own behaviors, emotions and thoughts in accordance with a particular situation. It involves filtering and modulating behavior. A good example of utilizing Self-regulation in communication is through the adoption of the one word Check-in, Check-out. While concise, it's incredibly effective in knowing where the people on the team stand. In contrast, dysregulation is what happens when there's a mismatch between the goals, responses, and modes of expression. An example would be if a person consistently used the one word Check-in to pontificate and take over "the floor". Self-regulation is the ability to calibrate your communication to serve your long-term interests and values.

In order to achieve optimal team outcomes, ideally, we as individuals and those on our teams will practice Self-regulation in our communication. Regulating our communication is a collective duty which reaps exceptional team benefits. Self-regulation honors those with whom you are communicating because it respects their time and recognizes their ability to absorb only so much information. By polishing your thoughts in line with goals and values, prior to speaking, you have given a gift to the listener. Because of your judicious use of the shared air space, listeners will be more desirous of spending time with you in the future because they have experienced this meaningful, behavioral respect that you've demonstrated to them through self-regulated communication.

Self-regulation requires clarity around long-term interests and the values of the team members. We might want to alter the amount or the volume of communication we share considering the long-term interests and values of our team. We may regulate the tone, the types of information we share and even the emphasis on our relationships. For example, one team we've worked with has a five-lines only email rule.

We can begin Self-regulating by considering the long view, knowing our teams' values and gaining deep knowledge about our own individual and collective emotional intelligence. In our teams, naming and honoring the importance of Self-regulation is essential to building psychologically safe, emotionally intelligent workplaces.

DEFINITION
Self-regulation:

The ability to monitor and control our own behaviors, emotions and thoughts in accordance with a particular situation.

WORKSHOP SELF-REGULATION:

Self-regulation entails filtering and consciously choosing what we communicate and with whom. Has a leader/teammate or partner ever suggested I alter the volume or content of what I communicate? What have I been told?

How can I modulate my communication in order to enhance the results of my relationships, while still being authentic and assertive?

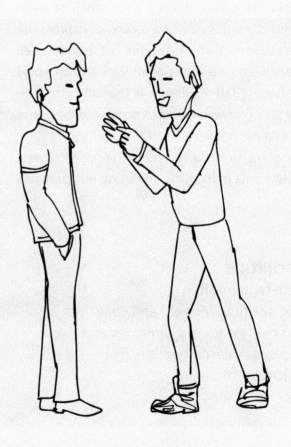

WEEK 9. RICHNESS OF MEDIUMS

"I can't text, ya know, I'm not charming via text. "

"Well, maybe you should stop texting."

"It's not just texting, it's email, it's voicemail, it's snail mail."

"That's regular mail."

"Whatever, none of it's working. I had this guy leave me a voicemail at work so I called him at home and then he emailed my blackberry and so I texted to his cell and then he emailed me to my home account and the whole thing just got out of control and I miss the days when you have one phone number, and one answering machine and that one answering machine housed one cassette tape and that one cassette tape either had a message from the guy or it didn't. Now I have to go around checking all these different portals just to get rejected by seven different technologies. It's exhausting."

— DREW BARRYMORE, THE 2009 FILM *HE'S JUST NOT THAT INTO YOU*

In the book *Perfect Pitch*, advertiser John Steel talks about the time his team was going to pitch Steve Jobs back in 1997. While waiting for Jobs to show up, two guys from Apple's marketing department bombarded the advertising team with an hour and a half, Death By Powerpoint, "agency briefing." Steel said, "Our presenter seemed oblivious to our pain; in the half light, he brought up slide after slide, graph after graph, table after table, each densely packed with numbers and with commentary he read verbatim." Not only is that boring, but it is the least rich medium to convey information.

Richness has to do with the amount of information a medium can convey. It depends on the availability of feedback, the use of multiple cues, the use of effective language, and the extent to which the communication has a personal focus. Face to face verbal communication is the richest medium. You use many cues, including voice, tone, facial expressions, and body language during a face to face interaction. Plus, with face to face you can more easily create a personal focus to your message.

Just when Steel and his colleagues thought they were going to pass out from boredom, Jobs came in, and got down to business. He turned off the projector, took a marker and drew over a dozen boxes on the dry erase board, then crossed out all but two. He explained that those two boxes represented the two projects he wanted Apple to work on (one was the iMac). Then he explained what he wanted from the ad agency and what message he wanted to craft for Apple users. Steel writes, "He had explained his strategy for the company in a little less than five minutes and he told us how he saw the role of communications in not much more than 60 seconds. The only visual aids he used were produced live using a marker and a dry erase board. Yet they seemed as vivid as any expensively produced slides or videos we've ever seen."

The impact Jobs had on that group of ad executives came through in how he engaged with them in an immediate way. He didn't need to rely on ironically enough, tech, but on his presence. It behooves us to consider our medium in our communication. **What will be the most effective?**

WEEK 9 ACTIVITY!

Color the picture below of the richness of mediums.

Here's the ranking of communication mediums from the richest to the least rich:

1. Face-to-face
2. Phone
3. Electronic messaging like e-mail or text
4. Personal written letters, notes or memos
5. Formal written reports or documents
6. Formal data analysis like graphs or statistical reports

You'll notice that the top three richest mediums are bi-directional in nature, when you are giving *and* receiving communication. Even if you are devoted to hand-written notecards and illustrated postcards, alas, that text message is still richer (but maybe not as artful or meaningful).

WORKSHOP RICHNESS OF MEDIUMS:

What is the communication medium I prefer the most when managing a difficult situation? Why?

A time when this medium was really beneficial:

A time when this preferred medium cost me:

A medium I want to try to use more:

MATCH THE MEDIUM WITH HOW YOU INTEND TO COMMUNICATE DURING FUTURE SITUATIONS LIKE THIS.

▶ My partner is consistently ignoring my texts.

▶ My boss emailed and said they need to talk to me.

▶ My best friend's partner just broke up with them.

▶ My employee is doing a crap job.

▶ My boss gave me a poor review on a project I thought was fantastic.

▶ My grandmother sent me a sweater.

▶ My boss' boss wants to hear about the progress of my team's big project.

▶ I want to schedule dinner with a busy friend.

▶ TEXT

▶ FACE TO FACE IN AN OFFICE

▶ PHONE CALL

▶ PRESENTATION (prezi or powerpoint)

▶ HANDWRITTEN NOTE

▶ EMAIL

▶ WRITTEN REPORT

▶ FACE TO FACE OVER COFFEE

WEEK 10 ACTIVITY!

Color the picture below of Empathy and
Deep Perspective-taking.

WEEK 10. EMPATHY AND DEEP PERSPECTIVE TAKING

"I think we all have empathy. We may not have enough courage to display it."

— MAYA ANGELOU

"When you show deep empathy towards others, their defensive energy goes down, and positive energy replaces it."

— STEPHEN COVEY

Empathy is not just the ability to feel another's feelings but also the ability to recalibrate our behaviors based on the other person's feelings. Empathy is a critical dimension of emotionally intelligent communication because it allows us to quickly connect with another person by establishing our shared humanity in our difficulties. Our own imperfection and woundedness allows us to put ourselves on the same team, in the same boat and in the struggle with the person across from us. Empathy enables seemingly opposing parties to focus on creating mutually beneficial solutions.

Empathy plays a significant role in Emotional Labor which requires us to regulate our emotions as part of our job duties. Our emotions become commodities. In the 1999 comedy "Office Space," Jennifer Aniston's waitress character gets in trouble for not having enough "flair" on her uniform for

Empathy also de-escalates conflict and opens new boundaries and collaborative contacts where there might be a lack of trust or perceived threat.

work. To be a successful server at Chotchkie's, she was expected to radiate enthusiasm and fun at all times while on the clock. That took a toll and she eventually quit the job.

In the world of Emotional Labor, the difference between Surface Acting and Deep Acting is key. Surface Acting looks like pretending to be enthusiastic and/or suppressing emotions (aka, "shining it on"). But Deep Acting is a process where employees change their internal feelings to align with organizational expectations, producing natural displays of emotion. Not surprisingly, Deep Acting produces greater employee engagement and organizational well-being than Surface Acting. We work with a local organization that does meaningful work to help refugees. Despite frustration over legislation blocking their efforts, the people in that organization are bonded by their shared mission. Instead of burning out, they are experiencing renewed resolve to help the people they are committed to serving.

Deep Acting is greatly enhanced and accelerated by taking the perspective of the client, customer, student or patient. Perspective-taking and empathy require understanding the situation from the other person's point of view. Empathy reduces feelings of anger towards the other. Research has repeatedly demonstrated that while surface acting causes emotional exhaustion on the job, empathy and deep acting create positive results for the employee and, for example, in the healthcare field, better quality of care for patients and enhanced mental health for physicians. Empathy also de-escalates conflict and opens new boundaries and collaborative contacts where there might be a lack of trust or perceived threat. Atticus Finch in *To Kill a Mockingbird* says that, "You never really understand another person until you consider things from his point of view, until you climb into his skin and walk around in it."

There are also three concrete tools that can help you become more empathetic.

❶ The first tool is **mindful listening,** which you learned about already. Remember that you are not just listening to what's being said, but most importantly, what's NOT being said.

❷ You can also start using the technique of **'looking for the human behind every thing.'** For example, when you have your coffee in the morning, think about that person who picked those beans. What's her morning like? Or as you button your shirt, think about the person who sewed on those buttons. Being curious about the people behind the object strengthens our empathy muscles.

❸ A third concrete tool for boosting your empathy is to be **curious about strangers.** You can even interact with them. Talk to them about their lives, their kids, their joys and you will feel how closely connected we are.

There's been a great deal of interest in empathy in recent years, even with an Empathy Museum opening in London in 2015. As Daniel Goleman, one of the fathers of Emotional Intelligence said, "Without empathy, the listener is tone deaf."

WEEK 10 ACTIVITY!

We can learn to empathize in our behavior and our communication. To get a baseline of your current ability, you can take the empathy assessment by neuropsychologist, Simon Baron Cohen called "Reading the Mind in the Eyes." Go online and search the *New York Times'* October 3, 2013 article "Can You Read People's Emotions" and take the assessment.

WORKSHOP EMPATHY AND DEEP PERSPECTIVE TAKING:

How can I incorporate empathy into my workplace interactions?

Here are three ways I can improve my own empathy to improve communication in my professional life.

1.

2.

3.

I remember an important time when a colleague expressed empathy and it deepened our relationship:

When others are empathetic toward me, I feel:

There are a couple of things that make it difficult for me to put myself in the shoes of another person.

1.

2.

Watch Brené Brown's video on Empathy at https://youtu.be/1Evwgu369Jw (or search "Brené Brown on empathy The RSA" on Youtube): How does Brown distinguish between empathy and sympathy?

I will adopt two new empathetic behaviors including:

1.

2.

Psychologically Safe Communication

WOULD YOU BELIEVE THAT SATURDAY NIGHT LIVE is run by a guy who is all about psychologically safe communication? Executive Producer, Lorne Michaels will check in with his people, the writers and actors, especially if they seem bothered or distracted. Everyone on the team is important and everyone has a voice, so if somebody seems off, Michaels will stop the meeting to focus on the issue. Research shows that teams with psychological safety are able to achieve better outcomes because they aren't afraid to joke around, be vulnerable, make mistakes, and take greater risks. Creativity and innovation can flourish. The following practices help foster psychological safety in teams.

WEEK 11: GROUND RULES

WEEK 12: ROUGH DRAFT

WEEK 13: THE SPEAK-NOW-OR-FOREVER-HOLD-YOUR PEACE RULE

WEEK 14: NON-TRIANGULATION/DIRECT NEGOTIATION

WEEK 15: APPRECIATIVE COMMUNICATION

Color the picture below of Ground Rules.

WEEK 11. GROUND RULES

"If you paint in your mind a picture of bright and happy expectations, you put yourself into a condition conducive to your goal."

— NORMAN VINCENT PEALE

Ground rules create a set of clear expected behaviors setting the norms for the life of a team or even just during a meeting. Ground rules are typically established with input from all of the participants at the beginning of the meeting or during the forming of a team. The facilitator explains the goal of the ground rules first, which is usually to create a safe environment, to keep

DEFINITION
Ground Rules (according to MIT):
Systems that are used by teams to define the way the team members will work together. Ground rules also establish boundaries for the team; they specify how the members will act when completing the project. Ground rules should be clear and specific and not general or ambiguous.

focus on the agenda or to facilitate ideation. Team members are asked to share concrete suggestions for behaviors that will enhance the outcomes of the group. They may be written on a chalkboard, whiteboard or flipchart and all of the members of the group consider and digest the list. Once the list is created, the facilitator asks all the team members

if they are comfortable with adopting the rules. If not, they can edit until the group is satisfied. Once accepted, the facilitator asks everyone to commit to the ground rules. An enforcer, someone other than the leader, can be selected to enforce the rules so that the leader can focus her attention on the agenda.

Ground Rules can be used to enhance the following systems:

▶ For meetings
▶ For dealing for conflict inside and outside the team
▶ For dealing with unmet expectations
▶ For project planning
▶ For communicating with each other

A few examples of Ground Rules:

▶ Everyone is responsible for enforcing ground rules.
▶ All meetings will begin and end on time; no session will run longer than 2 hours.
▶ Proceed as long as there is a majority of the team present.
▶ No phone calls—emergency interruptions only.
▶ Minimize or eliminate side conversations.
▶ One person will speak at a time.
▶ While generating ideas, withhold debate and criticism.
▶ Treat everyone's ideas with respect.
▶ Suspend judgment until everyone has been heard.

- While disagreeing or debating, focus comments on the facts and not on personalities.
- Avoid using acronyms unless known by everyone.
- If we reach an impasse, use the "Parking Lot."
- Try to reach consensus on key decisions, but don't rush.
- Speak from the heart.
- We all must be able to support and defend all major decisions that go out from this group.
- Read agenda before attending meeting.
- Give advance warning to all parties if you will be absent or late for a meeting.
- Be concise, don't waste time in meetings by repeating what has already been said or is irrelevant.
- Reserve judgment.
- Only one minute tangents are allowed.

WORKSHOP GROUND RULES:

The most unproductive behavior that occurs during meetings in my workplace is:

I think maybe this behavior persists because:

What would happen if my team stopped that behavior?

3 Ground Rules which would create the norms to prevent this behavior might be:

1.

2.

3.

An upcoming meeting when I can use Ground Rules might be:

Two things I can do to prepare myself and my team to optimally use Ground Rules might be:

1.

2.

WEEK 12 ACTIVITY!

Color the picture below of the team needing the Rough Draft concept.

WEEK 12. ROUGH DRAFT

At a nearby Buddhist monastery...

"Said a disappointed visitor, 'Why has my stay here yielded no fruit?'"

"Could it be because you lacked the courage to shake the tree?"

— *ONE MINUTE WISDOM*, ANTHONY DE MELLO

In order to be innovative and creative, we need to feel that our ideas won't be shot down immediately. At IDEO, the design company, the first rule of brainstorming is "no judgment." Wild ideas are encouraged and always have been. Years ago before the "mouse" was invented, Steve Jobs went to Xerox for a design which would have cost the consumer $1,200. He tried Hewlett-Packard. Their design only cost $150 but would take three years to make. Probably frustrated, Jobs approached

> **To come up with really creative ideas, we have to just get something down.**

IDEO. In less than a month, the IDEO team had something workable. "We made the outside from a Walgreen's butter dish. It cost $17 to make," David Kelley, IDEO's president said. The mouse was born.

At Work Wisdom, we are interested in what already works for teams. During a training with the Women's Center at Franklin & Marshall College, one student offered a suggestion that worked with her former team. Before giving a suggestion that hadn't already been thought through completely, team members would say, "Rough draft, what if we..." and float their idea. Daniel Goleman in his book, *Emotional Intelligence* says if you don't

feel you like you have to filter an idea, you can be more creative. We adopted the tool immediately and love it. It's easy and especially helpful for perfectionists who might normally stay silent. It allows people to loosen up a little.

To come up with really creative ideas, we have to get something down. Later we can work it over. Author Anne Lamott wrote, "Almost all good writing begins with terrible first efforts. You need to start somewhere. Start by getting something-anything-down on paper. What I've learned to do when I sit down to work on a sh!*%y first draft is to quiet the voices in my head." At Work Wisdom, we've gotten to an organizational norm where we advance crazy ideas all the time. This very workbook was a rough draft idea.

WORKSHOP ROUGH DRAFT:

This week you're going to experiment with Rough Draft. We want you to grow in comfort with this tool so we'll start easy by having you try it out first on family or friends.

The idea I have that I've been wanting to present at HOME but haven't is:

I haven't presented the idea because:

I could utilize Rough Draft at HOME to make it easier to present ideas by:

The idea I have that I've been wanting to present at WORK but haven't is:

I haven't presented the idea because:

I could utilize Rough Draft in my workplace to make it easier to present ideas by:

WEEK 13. THE SPEAK-NOW-OR-FOREVER-HOLD-YOUR-PEACE RULE

"A lot of people are afraid to say what they want.
That's why they don't get what they want."

— MADONNA

A large haircare and beauty product company was having lots of problems trying to be productive as a team. Stress was running high, because profits were not great and they were in danger of bankruptcy. One significant problem was that when decisions were being made, they were ruminated about for many weeks and months long after the fact. This habit of "Monday morning quarterbacking" created ill-will and paranoia among team members. An outside observer was able to pinpoint this problem and suggested they create something like *Speak-Now-or-Forever-Hold-Your-Peace*. The rule posits that after a certain number of days or weeks, the team would choose to **stop** picking apart a decision after the fact. Instead of ruminating about why that decision was made, they would have had time to give their feedback. After a certain amount of time, the window to give an opinion would close, a decision would be reached and everyone would accept it and move forward.

Speak-Now-or-Forever-Hold-Your-Peace promotes the creation of solutions, of improvements and of evolution. And it helps teams focus on embracing the new normal.

Once implemented, the practice brought harmony within the ranks at this beauty care company. And not only did they save money, they were able to rebound and avoid bankruptcy. A psychologically safe culture emerged and made the difference in their success.

Adopting the Speak-Now-or-Forever-Hold-Your-Peace rule helps remind people to speak up if they disagree or have different ideas. After a decision has been made, and there's been a bit of time for it to really absorb, everyone can move in the same direction of adoption and execution.

WEEK 13 ACTIVITY!

Color the picture below of co-workers following the
Speak-Now-or-Forever-Hold-Your-Peace-Rule.

WORKSHOP THE SPEAK-NOW-OR-FOREVER-HOLD-YOUR-PEACE RULE:

A time when my team made a decision to move forward with a new plan, policy or venture and there was full commitment from the team:

A time when there was not unanimous support of a new initiative but rather dissention that continued long after the policy was adopted and implemented:

What would happen if we adopted this rule at our organization?

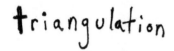

WEEK 14. NON-TRIANGULATION

"When it comes to gossip, I have to admit men are as guilty as women."

— MARILYN MONROE

"Direct confrontation, direct conversation is real respect."

— PENN JILLETTE

Triangulation is a behaviour that we discovered in the research from the field of Family Therapy. Triangulation is a manipulation tactic where one person will not communicate directly with another person, but takes the message to a third person, thus forming a triangle. Perhaps you've experienced when two people are having some conflict with each other and one of them chooses to bring you in as a third party by either 'processing' this conflict or trying to pit you against the other individual. This attempt is often made to persuade the

DEFINITION

Triangulation:

a manipulation tactic where one person will not communicate directly with another person, but takes the message to a third person, thus forming a triangle.

third party of rightness or wrongness, or to malign character. The triangle does not help in solving the root problem. Typically the issue is between two individuals in conflict and they're the ones best positioned, with the most insight into how the problem can be ultimately solved. Granted, there are times when a third party is absolutely necessary and helpful (legal claims, mediation), but very

often including a third party is not helpful and only erodes the trust between the original two parties, making subsequent healing of the relationship much more difficult.

Non-triangulation (also called Direct Negotiation) encourages the two original parties to speak directly with each other and negotiate a mutually satisfying outcome. If those two individuals are open, and using communication that helps them illuminate the real issues, they are more likely to reach a collaborative solution to their conflict.

To discourage the practice of excessively involving an outside third party, adopting a policy of non-triangulation encourages a culture of direct negotiation. When the time comes that one of the people in the conflict approaches a third-party to pull them into the discussion, that third-party can concisely, professionally and firmly redirect the triangulating party back to the person with whom they're having a conflict by saying something along the lines of, "You two have the skills to work this out." As mentioned, there are certainly occasions when grievances need to be filed. A third-party neutral may need to be involved in a formal investigation of harassment or some other organizational injustice but many times triangulation doesn't warrant a third-party.

You and your organization may consider adopting Non-triangulation on a pilot or permanent basis and evaluate its usefulness in solving problems and building trust in the culture and climate of the organization.

We've also created a practice called Positive Triangulation, which is intentionally talking behind the backs of colleagues in a positive way. Stephen Covey suggested that if you are talking about someone who is not in the room, PRETEND that they are present. One's language becomes gentler and more constructive by adopting this practice of pretend-presence. Positive Triangulation will inevitably circle back to the person. It also has the by-product of instilling norms for laudable behavior into the culture. If I talk about my colleague's resourcefulness and courage, I'm uplighting and promoting these features of her exemplary behavior. This will make her feel engaged and encouraged, but will also make me and others inspired to be resourceful and courageous. Our ultimate goal is to flourish and to help others flourish, and Positive Triangulation is an effective means to that end.

DEFINITION
Positive Triangulation: intentionally talking behind the backs of colleagues in a positive way.

WORKSHOP NON-TRIANGULATION:

There was a particularly difficult conflict I had with another individual in my workplace. In summary, this happened:

The cost of that situation was:

Now that I know about Triangulation, Non-Triangulation and Positive Triangulation, if I had a do-over button, I may have done this instead of how I originally communicated:

I may be Triangulating in this current situation:

I could do these three things so that I could embrace Non-Triangulation with my team:

1.

2.

3.

I can think of three people about whom I want to Positively Triangulate.

PERSON	THE AMAZING THING I SHOULD TALK ABOUT BEHIND THEIR BACK

Explain what you think the difference is between seeking counsel and trash talk. How are the motives different? How are the tones different? How are the outcomes different?

Trash Talk Turn around

by Sarah Colantonio & Kedren Crosby

ACT I TRIANGULATION

Acme Inc

"Hey Dorothy. Sorry I was slow today!"

Dorothy and Arthur leave work at the end of the day.

"I saw the boss pull you aside. Everything okay?"

"Hey Arthur. Yep. See you tomorrow"

Dorothy heads off to her car.

"See ya"

"? ok..."

Arthur leaves.

"How was work today?"

"Ugh. I can't stand working with Arthur. He slows everybody down. We're so slammed right now and running behind. I wish I could light a fire under his butt!"

"Geez"

Dorothy runs into Jack in the parking lot.

Dorothy vents her frustration about Arthur to Jack.

"uh huh yea, totally"

End of Act I

WEEK 15. APPRECIATIVE COMMUNICATION

"We need to discover the root causes of success rather than the root causes of failure."
— DAVID COPPERRIDER

"We live in the world our questions create."
— DAVE, AGAIN

*"Positive questions bring out the best in people, inspire positive action,
and create possibilities for positive futures."*
— DIANA WHITNEY

At 10 p.m., Kedren called me from South Carolina. "My flight was delayed so much that I missed my connecting flight to Philly. I won't be able to make it to the conference in the morning to give my presentation. I need you to do it." After several heart attacks, we hammered out the details and I was set to speak. In the end, ten minutes before her talk was scheduled to start, she strolled in. We co-presented and it ended up being kind of fun. But afterwards we said, what did we learn from this? How can we do better? I said, "When traveling, schedule a day between gigs in case of delays." She said, "Better sneakers to be able to run faster in the airport." Appreciative Communication allows us the opportunity to focus on the positive. What do I do best? What can we gain from this experience? How can I improve on my performance?

DEFINITION
Appreciative Communication:
Talking about a vision that's possible rather than analyzing the problem or talking about what is not possible.

Appreciative Communication comes out of the field of Appreciative Inquiry which is an approach to organizational change based on strengths rather than on weaknesses. It's this idea of talking about a vision that's possible rather than analyzing the problem or talking about what's not possible. David Cooperrider is the father of Appreciative Inquiry.

Here are some principles that build Appreciative Communication:

▶ First, you want to spend time talking about what gives you energy because the more you focus on your energy and your strengths, the more those increase.

▶ The second principle is to focus on what you want to achieve rather than what you don't want to achieve. That's more effective than focusing on solving a problem. You want to raise your gaze and focus on what *could* be rather than what we need to problem-solve.

▶ A third part of Appreciative Communication is about wanting to discover strengths. Be curious about what each other's strengths are. Be curious about the collective team strengths. Asking questions to get you to these strengths is a helpful form of Appreciative Communication.

▶ People also enjoy storytelling which is a helpful tool in embedding identity into your organization. As you're discerning those strengths, you can listen for pivotal stories that you can put on heavy rotation so that they can embed in the minds of others the kind of culture that you want to have in your organization. You may ask your team "when are we our best?" and retell those stories to people who are new to the team so that everyone has a sense of the team's superpowers. It builds momentum and also helps instruct people on the kinds of behavior that will be rewarded.

▶ With Appreciative Communication, think about how you deal with failure. There will be times when things don't go as planned and it's important to autopsy the failure in a constructive way so that you're looking into the "cadaver" of that failure. Get serious about what is wrong, and ask, "what is there about what happened that we can change so the next time this occurs, we will do something differently?" Always see failure in an appreciative light, in a way where you are going to look through the process, look through the sequencing and see what can be done better next time.

Use these tools of Appreciative Communication and you will find that by looking at what can be, in this very positive light, it will give you greater effectiveness in accomplishing what you want to accomplish. But you'll also have more joy, organizational well-being and more employee engagement along the way.

WORKSHOP APPRECIATIVE COMMUNICATION:

Asking questions of others opens them to positive possibilities while also empowering them how to process and problem-solve. What is an area of my current work where I want to help others discern, discover and dream?

What question(s) can I ask of others that will enable them to recall and relive a time of strength on my team?

How can I retell, animate, repeat, relive these appreciative stories in ways to ingrain new employees with my team's identity of strength?

The superpowers of each of my teammates are:

My own superpower is:

When I think of my biggest career failure, in what way am grateful for that failure because of the positive consequences that resulted?

How can I communicate to my team that each failure contains data to be mined for the enhancement of future successes?

THE FOURTH DIMENSION

Collaborative Communication

COLLABORATIVE COMMUNICATION requires a bidirectional exchange of information to harness the collective brilliance of a team. Collaborative communication also requires assertiveness and clarity. It requires the ability to state what you want as well as offer curiosity and discerning about what the other party wants. True collaboration melds the interests of the self and the other together to craft a mutually satisfying outcome. Collaborative communication seeks to build cohesion that allows for dissent so that teams may have the broadest perspectives and most creative ideas in their marketplace.

WEEK 16: CONVERSATIONAL TURN-TAKING

WEEK 17: THE GAP

WEEK 18: ORGANIZATIONAL CONVERSATION

WEEK 19: KNOW YOUR CONFLICT STYLE

WEEK 20: AUTHENTIC PERSUASION

Color the picture below of Conversational Turn-taking

WEEK 16. CONVERSATIONAL TURN-TAKING

"The perfect metaphor for teams is a see-saw, not a sports team."

— EDGAR SCHEIN

This practice might conjure the hippie image of chilled out folks using a talking stick around a camp fire to take turns talking, but it is effective around the conference table, or the dinner table. And it doesn't require an actual talking stick.

Google's Project Aristotle examined what makes teams extraordinary. A practice that was observed across the board was the even amount of input in conversation by all the team members. No one person dominated discussion. Everyone had the opportunity and was expected to share equally.

This can have several positive outcomes, one of which is better employee engagement. Many companies wonder how to instill motivation in their workers but an organic way to achieve this is to have everyone involved. Members are more likely to be engaged if they have skin in the game, if they had a part in implementing a new idea or plan. If our name is on something, we care about what happens to it. There's more ownership. And if that's the expectation in a team, that everyone has to contribute, then everyone is working harder to come up with the best possible ideas, the greatest way to achieve something, the simplest most beneficial solution. Members are happier with outcomes that they were involved with, even if it means compromising and giving up some of their preferences.

The other benefit is it illuminates team members who might be unhelpful. If all members are part of the process and will be heard from, and at every meeting one person is consistently noncommittal or without an opinion, that will be noticeable. And not in a good way. A famous pit fall of small groups is the "moocher". This is a team member who gets the accolades and benefit of being in a productive group but doesn't do much to contribute. Conversational turn-taking highlights the "moocher" by either motivating them to work harder or illustrating that they don't fulfill the group expectation to work hard towards a common goal.

At first, a leader might be the enforcer the Conversational Turn-taking. In a group of people, with all kinds of preferences, experiences, and personalities, especially an introverted person might opt out of giving an opinion or sharing information. If someone is in a bad mood or insecure, they might not share. Over time, as the team leader continues to enforce this norm, other team members will chip in and help make this the standard protocol for team meetings.

Practicing Conversational Turn-taking requires many of the other Authentic Communication practices, like Mindful Listening, the Pause Practice, and Self-Regulation.

If you assemble a team because you think they're brilliant, innovative and interesting, this is a vital practice. Leverage their brains and perspectives. The kinds of ideas that can emerge from many great minds playing off each other is exciting to consider. And it's essential for collaboration.

WORKSHOP CONVERSATIONAL TURN-TAKING:

How is the collective participation in conversation during team meetings?

Does anyone dominate the conversation?

Is there a person who never speaks up?

How can I ensure Conversational Turn-taking on my team?

What will this require of me?

When will I start?

What benefits do I foresee by practicing Conversational Turn-taking with my team?

WEEK 17 ACTIVITY!

Color the picture below of THE GAP.

WEEK 17. THE GAP

"Treat those who are good with goodness, and also treat those who are not good with goodness. Thus goodness is attained. Be honest to those who are honest, and be also honest to those who are not honest. Thus, honesty is attained."

— LAO TZU

"If an offense come out of the truth, better is it that the offense come than that the truth be concealed."

— THOMAS HARDY, *TESS OF THE D'URBERVILLES*

Authentic Communication teaches us to give feedback and receive feedback in a constructive manner. Often these conversations are related to accountability. They often come down to disappointments in each other, and addressing how we adopt new behaviors that are going to improve outcomes for our organization.

A practice that we have found to be very successful for ourselves and our clients is called *"The Gap"*. First, you describe what the expectation is upfront. You need to have clarity around the goal and how that goal is going to be accomplished. In a conversation with a colleague you might talk about some report that you're asking a colleague to submit to you. You're going to want to describe exactly what the report needs to include, as well as when is it due, how you want that report delivered to you, along with any other characteristics that are part of your expectations.

By laying out the expectations up front, there is less room for error. Let's say that you have an expectation that your colleague would submit a report to you on Friday. You might say to her, *"Hi Sarah, how are things? Can you give me that P&L by this Friday at 5 o'clock, close of business. Can you email that and by the way, it's the P&L that has the blue background."* You can be specific with her about which P&L you're hoping to get. Then you say to her, *"Does that work for you?"* and she can tell you, *"Yes, absolutely that works for me."* or she can say, *"Actually, I'm on vacation on Friday. I'll either have to get it to you on Thursday or Monday."* You two can negotiate whether it needs to be Thursday or Monday but the real clarity is around when that P&L needs to be submitted to your inbox. Let's say Monday is what you decide. Monday comes and goes. There's nothing in your inbox. It is Wednesday until you get a chance to talk to Sarah. The conversation might go something like this, *"Sarah, I'm wondering, did you submit that P&L? I*

DEFINITION

The Gap: The space between what the agreed upon expectation was and what happened. The Gap is when you have laid out clear expectations with a team member to complete a particular task and they have accepted the responsibility for that task but then do not fulfill their end. When you provide feedback regarding the uncompleted task or unfulfilled expectation, instead of blaming them, you point out "The Gap". It leads to problem solving on how to close the gap instead of defensiveness.

checked my inbox and I haven't seen anything. You may have submitted it but I haven't seen it." Then she could say, "Oh my goodness, I completely forgot about it." You can go on to describe this gap by saying, "Well, my expectation was that I would have it on Monday and it sounded to me like you were comfortable with that. It is now Wednesday and I don't have that P&L. We have this gap here. How are you going to close the gap?" Talking about The Gap and asking them how will they close The Gap is helpful because it's not judgmental. It's an inquiry and we know that questions help people become curious rather than defensive. By describing this Gap and asking them how they're going to close The Gap, you give them the opportunity to problem solve and they can suggest to you ways in which they want to close The Gap. If they land upon a solution for closing that Gap that is satisfactory to you, encourage them to go ahead and close The Gap. You might want to ask them "Going forward, how can we assure this gap doesn't occur again?" Again, there is no judgment on the person that they are somehow failing you or that there's anything bad about them. At this point you're simply talking about The Gap.

You can use this for any behavior in the workplace where you can talk about what the expectation is, what the reality is, that there's a gap between the expectation and the reality and send it back to that other person.

Giving and Receiving Feedback

In order to utilize The Gap, we have to be comfortable with giving feedback but also with receiving feedback. Some organizations are insightful in training their managers how to give feedback but almost no one trains their teams in how to receive feedback. But first, some helpful tips in how to give feedback.

First of all, it's helpful to have a self-check. You want to ask yourself, "Am I ready to give feedback from the right place?" For example, if we have been very disturbed and we're angry about some broken expectation, we might not be in the right place to give the feedback. See if you can get yourself into the right place so mentally you are able to give the feedback from a place that's going to be constructive to the other individual. You help that other person become a better, more effective employee, in this way.

Secondly, you can ask the employee, "Are you able to receive feedback at this time?" This question might be suitable for some organizational cultures more than others. This is an empathetic question. You are trying to gauge your listener. It may be that they only have five minutes. It may be that their dog has died. Maybe they are not open to receiving feedback because they received some other bad news. If they say, "No, I'm not able to receive feedback at this time," then you may say to them "How's tomorrow?"

You want to use empathy. You are trying to put yourself in their shoes and feel what they might be feeling. It's a helpful tool because you will have better advice for them if you understand where they're at.

Also, you want to pinpoint the problem. Too often when we give feedback, we're making generalizations about their behavior. We want to be as specific as possible so they will have clarity about how they can turn things around in the future.

Next, you want to lay out a path together for moving forward. You can use inquiry to ask them, *"How do you plan to move forward? Knowing what you know now, what sounds like a good plan for you?"*

Receiving Feedback

While all of us receive feedback almost daily and sometimes hourly, few of us have been taught how to optimally receive this data so it is as constructive and generative as possible. By following these five tips below you can open yourself to feedback that can create a better future for you. When we approach receiving feedback with a fixed mindset we view this data as criticism, because we believe that we are 'fixed' and unable to change. With a fixed mindset we see constructive input in a way that is negative and we often are defensive. If, on the other hand, we've opened ourselves to being curious and grateful for the opportunity to grow in increased self-awareness, we can hear with new ears the information that might be helpful to us. Receiving feedback well requires setting your mind and your intentions to openness, curiosity and even exploration. Because we know our self-communication sometimes is inaccurate, feedback is the vital reality testing that many of us need. Think of a bit of feedback that you received from a courageous colleague, friend or boss who cared enough about you to share something that ultimately made you grow. I will never forget my own incredulity when I was told that I was a catastrophizer (naturally I blew their feedback out of proportion). But now I can help myself if I slip into that unhelpful thinking.

Consider ways to adopt the five tips below for yourself and also to share them with your team, your children and anyone you care about who's also seeking ways to become a better version of themselves.

Use the exercises on the next page to practice using the tenants below for receiving feedback.

GIVING FEEDBACK

1. Self check: What is the purpose of the feedback? Am I ready to give it from the right place?

2. Ask, "Are you able to receive feedback at this time?"

3. Empathize

4. Pinpoint problems

5. Move forward

RECEIVING FEEDBACK

1. Be grateful for the opportunity to grow in self-awareness

2. Keep an open mind

3. Listen to understand, not to respond

4. Ask clarifying questions to get specific feedback

5. Analyze the feedback for usefulness and applicability

WEEK 17 ACTIVITY!

Find a partner for this verbal exercise. It can be anyone (colleague, friend, parent, boss, neighbor). For the first four statements, one of you plays the role of Giver and the other works to create responses according to the Tenets for giving and receiving feedback on the previous page. Switch roles for the second half of the exercise.

GIVER	RECEIVER
I feel like you aren't motivating your staff. They don't seem inspired.	Use Tenet ❸ to respond.
That meeting was longer than I expected.	Use Tenet ❹ to respond.
I spent three hours last night working on your evaluation so that I could give you detailed information.	Use Tenet ❶ to respond.
Has anyone ever told you that you talk too much during meetings?	Use any Tenet to respond.
I'd like to move you off this project. I think it's for the best for the company.	Use Tenet ❷ to respond.
You are absolutely worthless.	Use Tenet ❺ to respond.
You are absolutely worthless.	Use Tenet ❹ to respond.
I've noticed that you often don't make your deadlines for your monthly report.	Use Tenet ❸ to respond.

WORKSHOP THE GAP:

The issues of accountability that come up in my office are:

I can be more explicit and clear in communicating my expectations (verbally, nonverbally, in writing, etc.) by:

I can use "The Gap" to help my team be more successful by:

In reviewing the best practices for receiving feedback, the ones I want to enhance for myself are:

How will I do this?

Do you agree with this statement? "I will tell my supervisor/teammates that I'm working on certain behaviors and ask them to be my accountability partners."

(CIRCLE ONE)   **YES   NO   MAYBE   LET ME THINK ABOUT IT**

WEEK 18 ACTIVITY!

Color the picture below of Organizational Conversation.

WEEK 18. ORGANIZATIONAL CONVERSATION

"Just pay attention, then patch

A few words together and don't try

To make them elaborate, this isn't

A contest but the doorway

Into thanks, and a silence in which

Another voice may speak."

— MARY OLIVER, EXCERPT FROM THE POEM, *THIRST*

Imagine a conversation where you couldn't get a word in edgewise. That's not a conversation at all. That is someone talking *at* you. That person is likely enjoying the sound of their own voice, but they are missing out on the experience of real conversation, the back and forth, the mutual exchange. Similarly the old way of running a company is out. It is no longer a CEO standing on high and cacscading down messages to *his* direct reports and those direct reports send the message down to their direct reports and so on and so forth. In a book titled *Talk, Inc.* there are numerous case studies of how trusted leaders use conversation to power their organizations. In addition, an article in *Harvard Business Review* called "Leadership is a Conversation" concretely summarizes this idea: in order for communication to be truly effective, it needs to be more like a conversation. So how does this work? *Four ingredients: intimacy, interactivity, inclusivity and intentionality.*

❶ INTIMACY: promoting trust, mindful listening, and getting personal

Being congruent helps bring about trust. Mindful listening shows attention and respect. And getting personal does away with the barriers between the leaders and the employees.

One CEO had "listening sessions" where people could voice issues. One festering issue that came up was uneven compensation. Not only did he create the space to find out about the problem but then he did something about it.

Getting personal can take many forms but every organization needs to figure out how it will work best for them.

❷ INTERACTIVITY: promoting dialogue by utilizing practices like the Check-in and Check-out or The Platinum Rule

In a company where organizational communication is practiced, the CEO isn'tstanding on a stage with a microphone proclaiming their message. It's now about dialogue and exchange, adjusting the communication channels so that they are bidirectional. Work Wisdom adopted the use of Whatsapp so we have more immediate contact to share news with each other. Even if we aren't together in the office each day, we can still stay connected.

The Four Ingredients of Effective Organizational Conversations:

INTIMACY

INTERACTIVITY

INCLUSIVITY

INTENTIONALITY

❸ INCLUSION: Practicing Conversational Turn-taking and Authentic Persuasion

Brand ambassadors come from everywhere in the organization. A thought leader may use social media and email to promote their ideas through influence rather than authority. Opening up the dialogue means everyone's voice is heard and everyone has something to offer. It can range from making sure the quiet person in a meeting gets a chance to share to providing an open platform for employees to contribute ideas. When Work Wisdom holds our strategy sessions, we open it up to the floor. One participant started their comment with, "I'm sure you've thought of this..." and proceeded to give an interesting, new idea. Nope, we hadn't thought of it. But thankfully we had the platform to hear it.

❹ INTENTIONALITY: Explaining the why behind a decision or strategy

Maybe it worked well when we were children and our parents said, "Because I said so," but we're adults now and we all need to be intentional. Not by asserting strategic principles, but by explaining them and being open to having dialogue back and forth about how to make them better. A leader can explain why she has chosen the strategy she has, and maybe even be open to refining it and polishing it. Perhaps she might even redirect it based on the bidirectional, inclusive, intentional, intimate conversations that are happening in the workplace.

WORKSHOP ORGANIZATIONAL CONVERSATION:

How can my team and I authentically communicate with more: (concrete ideas)

INTIMACY

INTERACTIVITY

INCLUSION

INTENTIONALITY

The ways in which my organization is still hierarchical, cascaded and unidirectional are:

I want to leverage the techniques of organizational conversation to become a more powerful thought leader in my organization in these ways:

WEEK 19 ACTIVITY!

Color the picture below about managing conflict. Think about where you fall on the grid.

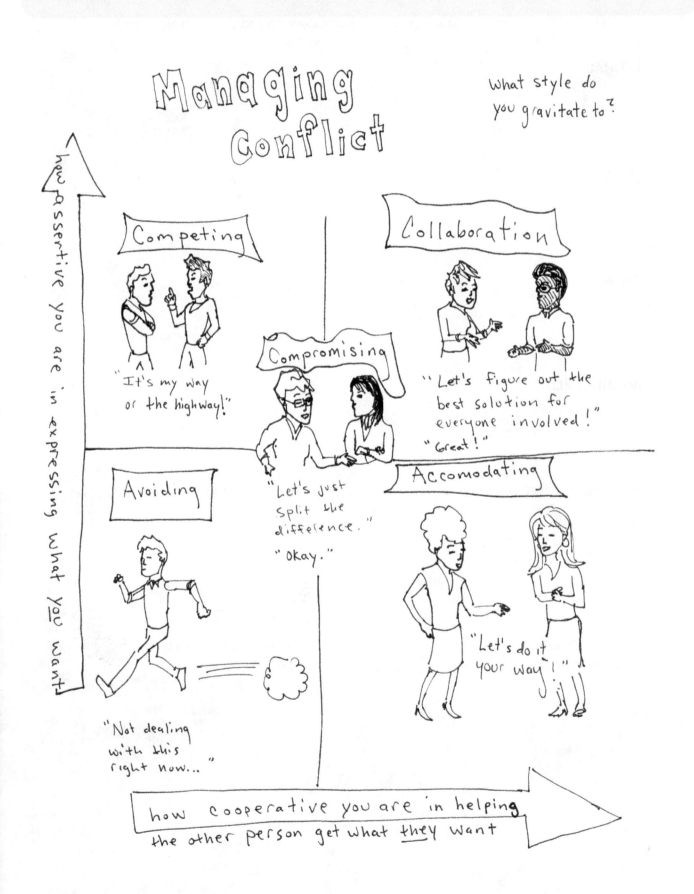

WEEK 19. KNOW YOUR CONFLICT STYLE

"I'd agree with you, but then we'd both be wrong."

— UNKNOWN

"Conflict is productive."

— PATRICK LENCIONI

I grew up in a house that couldn't handle conflict. On one side, we had fiery DNA and deep generational, cultural norms for rebel-rousing. On the other side we were famous white-knucklers, tight-lipped avoiders. These clichés don't do justice to the complexities and magnitude regarding how much we didn't deal with conflict. We struggled deeply as a "team" because we didn't understand the nature of managing differences, our own styles or each others'. And we certainly didn't celebrate each others' ways of managing differences. I figured that being alone in my room avoiding the battles, especially with a bag of fresh Lancaster County potato chips, was my destiny.

I was almost 30 years old when I enrolled in a class that focused on organizational conflict management. For the first time I was able to examine my family through this lens. Learning my own way of managing differences vastly changed my success, my "teams" and my BMI, too.

We hope this information works as well for you and your team, even if your team is your family.

Self-awareness is like jet fuel for adopting enhanced behaviors. A key behavior to predicting the effectiveness of a team or any relationship is how they manage conflict. Conflict doesn't hurt a team, but the way the team manages differences might. How do you deal with conflict?

We hope this information works as well for you and your team, even if your team is your family.

Knowing Your Conflict Management Predisposition

Directions: For each pair of statements, circle the one that sounds most like you.

1. a. Occasionally I hold back and let others figure out how to resolve the conflict.

   b. I aim to focus on similarities rather than differences in views.

2. a. I like to resolve problems through negotiating.

   b. I try to make sure everyone's concerns are addressed.

3. a. I know what I want and I go for it.

   b. I sometimes aim to make the other person feel better in order to end a conflict.

4. a. I like to resolve problems through negotiating.

   b. I'm willing to give up my own views if it will help the other person feel better.

5. a. I always try to work together to solve problems.

   b. I aim to avert uncomfortable situations when possible.

6. a. I do what I can to avoid tension.
   b. I aim to convince others that I am right.

7. a. I stall in order to take some time to think about problems before approaching them.
   b. I am willing to compromise when others do.

8. a. I know what I want and I go for it.
   b. I aim to discuss problems openly so that they can be worked out right away.

9. a. Sometimes conflicts are better left not discussed.
   b. I try to get what I want.

10. a. I know what I want and I go for it.
    b. I like to resolve problems through negotiating.

11. a. I aim to discuss problems openly so that they can be worked out right away.
    b. Sometimes I aim to make the other person feel better in order to end the conflict.

12. a. At times I keep my views to myself in order to avoid conflict.
    b. I prefer a "give and take" solution to problems where both sides make adjustments.

Almost finished...

13. a. If the other person can agree to disagree, I can do the same.

   b. I make sure others know my views.

14. a. I share my thoughts and ask others to share theirs.

   b. I aim to convince others that I am right.

15. a. I sometimes aim to make the other person feel better in order to end a conflict.

   b. I aim to avert uncomfortable situations when possible.

Don't Peek →

Answer Key

1. a. Avoider
   b. Accomodator

2. a. Compromiser
   b. Collaborator

3. a. Competer
   b. Accomodator

4. a. Compromiser
   b. Accomodator

5. a. Collaborator
   b. Avoider

2. 6. a. Avoider
   b. Competer

7. a. Avoider
   b. Compromiser

8. a. Competer
   b. Collaborator

9. a. Avoider
   b. Competer

10. a. Competer
    b. Compromiser

11. a. Collaborator
    b. Accomodator

12. a. Avoider
    b. Compromiser

13. a. Compromiser
    b. Competer

14. a. Collaborator
    b. Competer

15. a. Accomodator
    b. Avoider

What style(s) do you use most? _____

Knowing your style of managing differences builds authenticity and communication in your workplace. We each have a predisposition for how we manage differences, how we deal with conflict, how we manage collaboration. Anytime there are different interests (your own interest and then another person's interest) you have to discern how far you're going to push your own interests and how far you're going to cooperate with the other person's wants. You may be unassertive or very assertive in getting what you want. You may be uncooperative or very cooperative in satisfying the other party's interests. Throughout the course of the day, you may operate in all five different modes. None of these modes are good or bad. It's more important to notice your agility to move from one mode to another based on your situation. Seek to understand what the interests are, what the stakes are, the relational aspects of the communication, and where the power dynamics lie. Then we can choose the appropriate mode that will best serve us and best help the organization achieve what needs to be accomplished.

Let's dive a little deeper into the five modes for managing differences: competing, collaborating, compromising, avoiding and accommodating.

❶ COMPETING

Competing is both assertive and uncooperative. It is a power oriented mode. When you're competing, you're pursuing your own concerns at the other person's expense. You use whatever power seems appropriate in order to win your position. Competing might mean standing up for your rights, defending a position that you believe is correct or simply trying to win. Very often, if it's an issue of ethics or even safety you might operate in this mode. It's useful to have competing as a style when you need quick, decisive action like in an emergency. It is also helpful to go to competing when you have important issues with unpopular courses of action, like cost cutting and enforcing unpopular rules or discipline. It is helpful on issues vital to company welfare, when you know that you're right, around ethics, or when need to

THE FIVE MODES OF MANAGING CONFLICT:

❶ **COMPETING:** You want it the way you want it.

❷ **COLLABORATING:** This is where you and the other party work together to come to a mutually beneficial agreement. Collaboration takes effort, assertiveness, co-operation and problem solving. But it produces the happiest results.

❸ **COMPROMISING:** You and the other person each give in a little and each get a little of what you want.

❹ **ACCOMMODATING:** "We'll do it your way."

❹ **AVOIDING:** "I'm out."

protect yourself from people who take advantage of noncompetitive behavior.

You want to look for signs of overuse. If you are overusing competing as a conflict management style, you might be surrounding yourself with "yes" people or those who may be afraid to admit ignorance and uncertainties.

You might be under using competing. Think about if you feel powerless in situations, or if you sometimes have trouble taking a firm stand even when you see the need. If those things sound true to you, you may actually be under using this quadrant.

❷ COLLABORATING

The second style or mode is collaborating. Collaborating is both assertive and cooperative. You have to know what you want and be assertive in getting it. You have to know what the other party wants and you have to be cooperative in helping them get it. When you're collaborating, you attempt to work with the other person to find a solution that is fully satisfying to you both. You have to dig into the issue deep enough so that you can understand the underlying interests of both of you.

You'll want to use collaborating when you need to find an integrative solution and the concerns of both parties are too important to be compromised.

Collaborating is useful when you want to merge insights from people with very different perspectives on a problem, when you want to gain com-

mitment by incorporating other's concerns into a consensual decision or when you need to work through hard feelings.

A good example of our own collaboration came about when we decided we needed a new office for Work Wisdom. We could've gone to high competing. Sarah wanted something urban and modern and Kedren wanted something Parisian and grand. We almost came to fisticuffs by landing on certain spaces that were dramatically different, but then we decided to ask each other WHY we had in mind the visions we did. Sarah's underlying interest was in making our work feel fresh and innovative. Kedren's underlying interest was in making our clients feel warm and comfortable. We ended up in a very urban building with décor that is overstuffed, velvet, furry and French. It works because we collaborated by satisfying our underlying interests.

Signs of overusing collaboration might be that you sometimes spend time discussing issues to death that don't actually seem to warrant it. Collaboration takes a lot of time and energy and sometimes you can compromise. It takes a lot less time and energy than understanding everyone's interests and devising a mutually agreeable solution.

COLLABORATING may take the form of:
- ▶ exploring a disagreement to learn from each other's insights,
- ▶ confronting and trying to find a creative solution when resources are limited

Notice if your collaborative behavior fails to elicit collaborative responses from others. Do others to disregard or even take advantage of the trust and openness that you display?

Also you want to notice if maybe you're under using collaboration. Is it difficult for you to see differences as opportunities for joint gain, for joint learning, joint problem solving? Are others uncommitted to your decisions or policies? Maybe you didn't take the time to discern what their underlying interests are.

❸ COMPROMISING

The third mode to investigate is compromising. In compromising, your objective is to find an expedient, mutually acceptable solution that partially satisfies both parties. You're splitting the difference. Maybe you're doing it their way one day and your way the other day. You concede in order to reach middle ground quickly. Successful marriages use compromise often.

Compromise is the ideal mode when goals are moderately important but not worth the effort for the potential disruption involved in using more assertive modes. It's ideal when two opponents with equal power are strongly committed to mutually exclusive goals, or when they want to achieve a temporary settlement of a complex issue. If they need to arrive at an expedient solution under time pressure or as a backup mode when collaboration or competition fails, using compromise works best.

Signs of under use might be if you sometimes find it difficult to make concessions. Without this safety valve of compromise, you may have trouble gracefully getting out of mutually destructive arguments and power struggles.

One sign of overuse would be that you're concentrating so heavily on the practicalities and the tactics of compromise that you lose sight of larger issues. You might be neglecting issues like principles, values, or long-term objectives or company welfare. This can undermine building interpersonal trust and interpersonal relationships that are very important for the long run.

❹ AVOIDING

The fourth mode is avoiding. It's both unassertive and uncooperative. When avoiding, you don't immediately pursue your own concerns with the other person. You don't address the conflict. You don't work towards collaboration.

Avoiding might take the form of diplomatically side stepping an issue or postponing the issue until a better time. Or maybe it's withdrawing from a threatening situation when you feel like there's no way that you're going to win.

Times where it might be appropriate to use the avoiding style are as follows:

▶ Sometimes an issue is not really important.

▶ There are more important issues that are pressing.

▶ When you have no chance of satisfying your concerns.

- When you have no power or low power or you're frustrated by something that would be very difficult to change.

- When the potential costs of confronting a conflict outweighs the benefits of its resolution.

- When you need time to let people cool down, let cooler heads prevail, reduce tensions to a productive level again. To regain perspective and composure.

- When you have to gather more information. Tap the brakes long enough to delay an immediate decision.

- When others can resolve the issue more effectively than you can.

Notice if you're over using avoidance. Ask yourself, *"Does the team suffer because people sometimes have trouble getting my input on issue?"*

Maybe you're not being sufficiently assertive in sharing your point of view or your interests. Does it seem sometimes that people are walking on eggshells around you? It may be that there is a disproportionate amount of energy being devoted to caution and avoiding issues, indicating that those issues actually need to be faced and resolved. Are decisions on important issues sometimes made by default?

Avoiding is a useful tool that we often under use. Do you sometimes find yourself hurting people's feelings or stirring up hostilities? You might want to exercise more discretion and tact in framing issues in nonthreatening ways.

Do you sometimes feel overwhelmed by a number of issues? It may be that you're not avoiding enough. Maybe there are things that you could spend time avoiding and it may in fact lead to being less overwhelmed.

⑤ ACCOMMODATING

The fifth mode is accommodating. Accommodating is both unassertive and cooperative, the opposite of competing.

When you're accommodating, you sacrifice your own concerns in order to satisfy the current concerns of the other person. Accommodating might take the form of selfless generosity, charity, obeying another person's order when you really prefer not to, or maybe when you want to yield to the other person's point of view to ingratiate yourself to them.

Accommodating also has some relevant helpful uses. It's very effective when you:

- Realize that you're wrong.

- To allow a better solution to be considered,

- To learn from others and to show that you're reasonable.

- It's also useful when the issue is much more important to the other person than it is to you. This allows you to satisfy the needs of others, as a goodwill gesture to help maintain a cooperative relationship.

- It's helpful when you want to build up political capital for later issues that are important to you.

- When you're out-matched, losing and more competition only damages your cause. Accommodating can be useful to preserve harmony and avoid disruption.

- When you want to help your employees develop by allowing them to experiment and learn from their own mistakes.

Of course we also want to ask ourselves are we over using accommodating?

Are we turning into a martyr? When you feel that your concerns don't get the attention that they deserve, you might be deferring too much to the concerns of others. You can also ask yourself

if discipline is lax. Some rules and procedures are actually crucial. Accommodating on these issues may harm you and others and maybe even the organization.

Look for signs of under use. If you're having trouble building goodwill, it may be that you are under using accommodation. If you're viewed as unreasonable, you may be under using accommodation. You may have trouble admitting when you're wrong. You might fail to recognize legitimate exceptions to the rules, and if you're one of those who refuse to ever give up, maybe you should try using accommodation more often.

It's helpful when we know our own styles of managing differences because we're able to mitigate this natural disposition.

Learn your own conflict style. Ask questions of yourself. Grow in self-awareness and see whether or not you begin to operate differently in the workplace when it comes time to manage differences.

WORKSHOP CONFLICT STYLES:

Go back to your assessment and record your scores. If you score in the very high or low ranges of any of the modes, you will want to pay attention to how you use that mode. Consider whether or not you may be over using or under utilizing that style of managing differences. After you have absorbed the results of your report and noticed what style of conflict management you use, notice if you would like to use another mode more often.

The mode I use most often is:

The mode I would like to use more often is:

The mode I would like to use less often is:

I will do the following to accomplish that:

At work I overly rely on a particular style of managing differences:

a. Why am I choosing this mode?

b. How is this serving me well?

c. What is it costing me?

d. What if I chose another mode?

e. What will I communicate and to whom to achieve better results?

f. When will I communicate this?

WEEK 20. AUTHENTIC PERSUASION

"We're persuaded when we feel we've understood something well enough to make up our own minds. And that makes all of us smarter, better people, no matter what side of the issues (or the table) we're on."

— KC COLE

Authentic Persuasion is using our ability to influence for the well-being of our organization. We know it's important to be persuasive, we can make a lot of wonderful things happen if we can persuade people's attitudes and behaviors, but how can we really be effective?

The first persuasive tool to remember is to **know your audience. Know your audience. Know your audience.** The most effective persuaders know the needs, desires and values of the audience they want to persuade. In fact, an interesting *New York Times* article, "The Key to Political Persuasion" (November 13, 2018) validates this notion of knowing and speaking to the values of the audience in order to persuade. The authors relay a study which looked at politically conservative and liberal people and corresponding issues, i.e., gun rights and same sex marriage. When conservative people were presented the same sex marriage issue using language and reflecting the values of conservatives, they were significantly more likely to back the issue. And the same with liberals. If the gun rights issue was presented in liberal terms, liberals were statistically more likely to agree when their values were reflected in the argument.

The second thing to remember about authentic persuasion is to **be patient.** With all the persuasive messages out there, it's important to use critical thinking before holding fast to a position. So give your audience time to think it over. Those of us who are more thorough about our decision-making are going to follow through with our behavior.

Communication scholar Dan Rothwell uses this scenario to explain: Imagine you are on a date with an attractive person and when the waiter comes to tell you the specials, your date says they are vegan and gives explicit instructions on what they will eat. Your date turns to you and explains the horrors of the meat industry, the destruction of the planet from not eating vegan and suggests you should follow their lead. You aren't vegan

We know its important to be persuasive, we can make a lot of wonderful things happen if we can persuade people's attention, but how can we really be effective?

(yet) but you definitely want another date with this gorgeous creature so you say, "I'll have the same." Your date has chosen to eat the way they eat because they have given their decision quite a bit of thought. They have weighed the evidence and reasoning given and made a decision based on critical thought. You want a second date, you want them to like you, so you agree. Your behavior change is on the surface and likely will not be consistent.

Robert Cialdini is a noted persuasion expert and has identified a number of common persuasive shortcuts to keep in mind. You can watch his summary in the video on YouTube, *"The Science of Persuasion."* These elements of reciprocity, scarcity, authority, consistency, liking and consensus can be clarifying when we don't always realize why we are particularly persuasive with certain people or persuaded by a certain message or person.

Lastly, use the **Three-Act Persuasive Speech Structure.** Explain the current situation or problem. Make the cost of staying in that place clear. Next, present the solution, the way it could be if we implement this solution. Then show the resolution, "the new bliss". Illustrate how much better the organization will be with this transformation. As communication expert, Nancy Duarte in her book *Illuminate* says, "Audiences enjoy experiencing the dilemma and its resolution; it keeps them interested as you speak."

Using Authentic Persuasion is being aware of our power to influence, using influence responsibly, shedding the bad reputation persuasion has had since Plato, and using it for good.

WORKSHOP AUTHENTIC PERSUASION:

Take the Rokeach Values Survey (search **Rokeach Values Survey** and download the PDF list of **Terminal and Instrumental Values**). Give it to your team and find out what the top 5 values are for yourself and each member. Take notice of what the bottom three values are for yourself and others.

My top 5 Terminal Values are:

My top 5 Instrumental Values are:

The benefits to knowing the similarity and differences in the values of me and my team are:

The values and needs of my customers/clients/colleagues seem to be:

The way I learned about their priority values was through:

What benefits would come from knowing their priorities?

How could I learn that information?

RECAP:
THE 20 AUTHENTIC
COMMUNICATION PRACTICES

1. PARKING LOT

2. CONGRUENCE

3. THE PAUSE PRACTICE

4. MINDFUL LISTENING

5. AUTHENTIC SELF-COMMUNICATION

6. CHECK-INS, CHECK-OUTS

7. THE PLATINUM RULE

8. SELF-REGULATION

9. RICHNESS OF MEDIUMS

10. EMPATHY AND DEEP
    PERSPECTIVE TAKING

11. GROUND RULES

12. ROUGH DRAFT

13. SPEAK-NOW-OR-FOREVER-
    HOLD-YOUR-PEACE-RULE

14. NON-TRIANGULATION

15. APPRECIATIVE COMMUNICATION

16. CONVERSATIONAL TURN-TAKING

17. THE GAP

18. ORGANIZATIONAL CONVERSATION

19. KNOW YOUR CONFLICT STYLE

20. AUTHENTIC PERSUASION

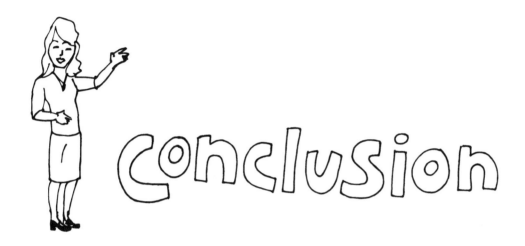

Conclusion

"Every great dream begins with a dreamer. Always remember, you have within you the strength, the patience, and the passion to reach for the stars to change the world."

—HARRIET TUBMAN

THEY SAY THAT YOU WRITE THE BOOK you need to read. This book grew out of a desire to become more Authentic Communicators ourselves. As with any healthy, helpful practice, (exercise, meditation, journaling, gratitude) it must be applied consistently to be transformative. While there is some benefit to simply learning the practices and adding the Authentic Communication vocabulary to your own, try selecting a few practices to use with deliberate intention.

When we work with teams, we ask them to select the tools which they believe will most significantly move the needle on the performance and well-being of themselves personally and for their teams.

Look over the list of twenty practices to the left. Circle the three which you believe will most significantly improve your own performance and well-being. Commit to experimenting courageously with them and weaving them into your communication.

Now look at the list again and consider your current team. Place checkmarks next to the three, if you adopted them, would bring high performance and well-being to your team. If you have been working through this workbook with your team, now is the time to compare notes on which tools they're prioritizing to see if there are common themes.

It's exciting and fun to work with a team that does good work, that is creative, innovative, and makes things happen. These practices can you help your team achieve that kind of greatness. So go forth and invent, problem-solve and make the world a better place using Authentic Communication!

Sources

Alix Spiegel, Hanna Rosin & Lulu Miller (journalists and podcasters)

Celeste Headlee (speaker and interviewer)

David Gelles (mindfulness)

Daniel Goleman (emotional intelligence)

Amy Edmonson (psychological safety)

Julia Wood (communication scholar)

Dan Rothwell (communication scholar)

Brené Brown (qualitative researcher)

Byron Katie (mindfulness)

Anthony De Mello (mindfulness)

Tara Brach (mindfulness)

Adam Grant (author, speaker, organizational behavior)

Stephen Covey (leadership)

David Copperrider, Suresh Srivastva and Diana Whitney (Appreciative Inquiry)

Kerry Patterson, Joseph Grenny, Ron McMillan and Al Switzler (communication)

Michael Slind and Boris Groysberg (leadership)

Robert Cialdini (author, persuasion expert)

Dana Morris-Jones (conflict management)

Charles Duhigg (journalist and author)

Nancy Duarte (conflict management)

Jon Steel (marketing)

Ralph Kilman (conflict management)

Michael A. Hitt, Adrienne Collella and C. Chet Miller (organizational behavior)

Martin Seligman (positive psychology)

SARAH COLANTONIO

With a Master's of Science in Communication and a Bachelor's in Psychology, Sarah has served as a professor of communication at both Millersville University of Pennsylvania and Penn State University since 2003. In addition to teaching communication, Sarah has practiced mindfulness since 2004 (yoga and meditation). She participated in trainings and certifications with Deepak Chopra, Tara Brach and Jack Kornfield. Sarah is a Certified Meditation Instructor (CMI). Her practice is heavily influenced by the teachings of Sharon Salzberg, Tara Brach, Bhante Gunaratana, Anthony De Mello and Osho.

KEDREN CROSBY

Kedren holds a Master's degree in Policy Science from The University of Maryland, graduate level Certificates in Nonprofit Studies from The Johns Hopkins University in Baltimore, Conflict Resolution at Notre Dame and has completed graduate coursework in Organizational Behavior at Harvard University. Kedren is also a certified practitioner of Emotional Intelligence and serves as adjunct graduate school faculty at Elizabethtown College. Kedren has written and presented extensively on burnout, work-life integration, authentic leadership, organizational culture, organizational conflict management and communication best practices.

Professionally, Kedren has enjoyed serving as a CEO, CDO, Director, Associate Director, Interim Executive Director, President, Vice President and professor. Her 25 years' workplace experience in all three sectors (for-profit, non-profit, government) fuel both her empathy and her practice which is rooted in authenticity, appreciative inquiry, crucial confrontations, emotional intelligence, positive organizational behavior, transformative mediation, positive psychology and the platinum rule.

CPSIA information can be obtained
at www.ICGtesting.com
Printed in the USA
BVHW061154130622
639649BV00010B/616